Copyright © 2016 by GM Publishers

Business Environment
Theoretical & Organizational Aspects

Author: Ghazi Mokammel Hossain

Designer: Ghazi Mokammel Hossain

Publications Format: Amazon Kindle E-Book format, Amazon Createspace Paper back format

Edition No: First Edition, July, 2016

Publication From: USA

Version: International Version

Published by: GM Publishers, associated with Amazon Kindle Direct Publishing & Createspace

ISBN-13: 978-1535042901
ISBN-10: 1535042907 (The book has been assigned a CreateSpace ISBN)

Email address: gmpublishers04@gmail.com

I0482180

GM Publishers
My Book My Life

Table of Contents

1.0 Introduction of the Contrasting Businesses Environments

Every business organization has different kinds of business environment. Some business organizations are operated for making profit and creating job opportunity for the jobless people. And some of the business organizations aren't operated for making profit (Hopkins, 2003). These types of organization don't focus on the profit building, they're operating their business for the development of the society, country and the world (Baye, 2000). So this types of business organizations maintain different business environments and different business strategies to obtain its objectives (Hopkins, 2003).

1.1 What is Business Environment?

Business environment of an organization is the combined forces of different factors like social, political, legal and economical etc. The factors affect the environment of the organization in different ways. All of these factors create an environment for the organization and it's called the business environment.

1.2 Different Types of Business Environment

There are mainly two types of business environment:
- Internal Environment
- External Environment

Internal Environment: Internal environment of business mainly based on the internal factors of the organization like value, objective, organizational structure, corporate culture, HRM etc. All of these factors play a vital role in the formation of internal environment.

External Environment: External environment of business is depended on the external factors that are micro and macro environmental factors. Micro and macro environments are main element of the external environment.

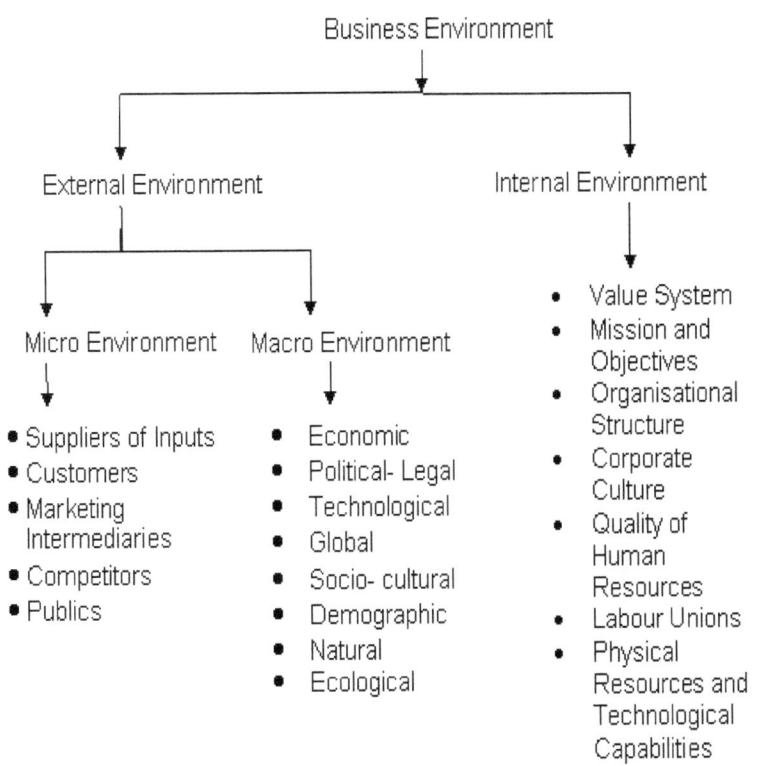

1.3 Features & Characteristics of Business Environment

Features of Business Environment:

1. Exchange of goods and services

2. Deals in numerous transactions

3. Profit is the main Objective

4. Business skills for economic success

5. Risks and Uncertainties

6. Buyer and Seller

7. Connected with production

8. Marketing and Distribution of goods

9. Deals in goods and services

   Consumer goods

   Producer goods

10. To Satisfy human wants

11. Social obligations

Characteristics of Business Environment:

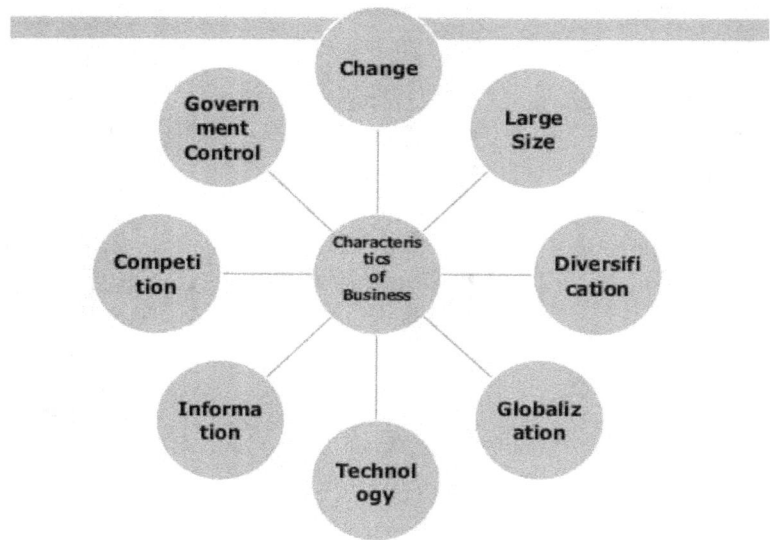

1.4 Importance of Business Environment

- Identification of strength
- Identification of weakness
- Identification of opportunities
- Identification of threats
- Exploitation of Business Opportunities
- Keeping business enterprise alert
- Keeping business flexible and dynamic
- Understanding future problems and prospects
- Making business socially acceptable
- Ensures survival and growth

1.5 Business Environment Drivers

The Changing Business Environment Business Drivers(Pressures)

- **Globalisation and Strong Competition**

  Management and control in a global marketplace, Competition in world markets, Global work groups, Global delivery systems

- **Transformation of Industrial Economies**

  Knowledge- and information-based economies, Productivity, New products and services, Knowledge: a central productive and strategic asset Time-based competition, Shorter product life Turbulent environment, Limited employee knowledge base

- **Transformation of the Enterprise**

  Flattening, Decentralization, Flexibility, Location independence, Low transaction and coordination costs, Empowerment, Collaborative work and teamwork

1.6 PESTAL Analysis of Business Environment

The word "PESTAL" is the combination of six different factors of business. The factors influence an organization's business environment locally and globally. The discussion of "PESTAL" is as follows:

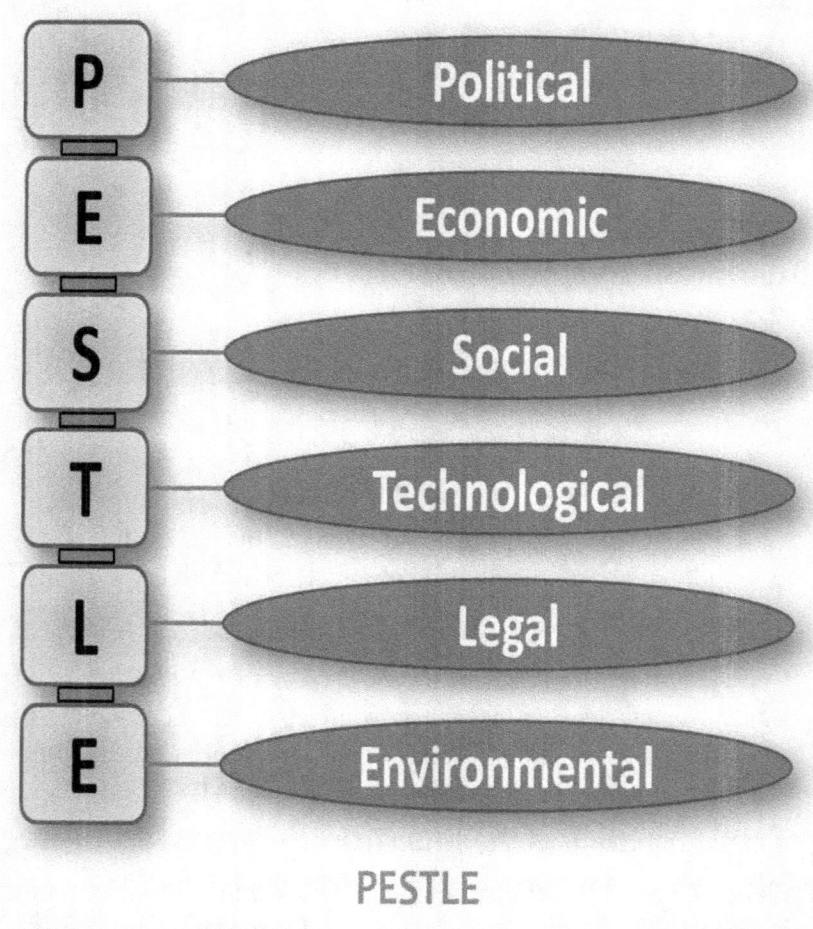

PESTLE

The PESTAL Analysis of the Business Organization:

POLITICAL	ECONOMIC	SOCIAL	TECHNOLOGICAL
• Regulatory bodies and processes • New government policies • Domestic and international activist and pressure groups	• Domestic and international economies • Taxation specific to services • Specific industry factors • Market routes and distribution trends • Customer/end-user drivers	• Lifestyle and social trends • Demographic shifts • Consumer attitudes and opinions • Media views • Brand and company image • Consumer buying patterns • Buying access and trends • Advertising and publicity • Ethical issues	• Competing technology development • R&D activity • associated/dependent technologies • Maturity of technology and adoption • Consumer buying mechanisms/technology • Intellectual property issues

1.7 Structure of the Analysis

In this book, we will discuss about the four different types of business organizations and their environments. In the first part, the discussion will be focused on Marks & Spencer (M&S) and The London School of Economics and Political Science's organizational and business environment. In the second part, the discussion will analyze the organizational and business environment of McDonald's and National Health Service (NHS). The research will also show the economic environment of Walmart, McDonald and distinguish it with M&S, KFC. It will also discuss the economic and business environment of major economy like China, UK, Germany, USA and EU.

The goal of this book is to provide real life scenarios and examples of renowned business organizations and its environments. It provides theoretical as well as organizational aspects of business environment. It's broadly provided the real life examples of different business organization's environment. As the overall discussions of the book are case study based, thus it will help a reader to easily understand about the business environment not only theoretically but also practically.

2.0 Identifying the Purposes of Various Organizations

Business organization has two important aspects, business policies, and strategies. These two aspects are mostly dependent on the various business operations performed by the organization. In this point of view, Marks & Spencer (M&S) and The London School of Economics & Political Science (LSE) or McDonald's and National Health Service (NHS) are operating different kinds of business for the local as well as the entire world. Four types of different business organizations with their purpose, aims and objectives are described below:

M&S and LSE's Business Environment Analysis

2.1 Marks & Spencer (M&S)

Marks & Spencer (M&S) is a very popular business organization in the UK and the entire world. Because this business organization not only run their business locally but operate their business globally (Baye, 2000). The business organization was established in 1884, the company is specialized in the selling of clothing, home products and luxury food products (Corporate.marksandspencer.com, 2015).

It is a major multinational retail business organization and its headquarter is located in the City of Westminster, London. In the year 1998, the company made a pre-tax profit of over £1 billion (Corporate.marksandspencer.com, 2015). Now the company's operating income in the year 2015 is £762.5 million and the total revenue is £10.3 billion. The aims and objectives of M&S are given below:

2.2 Aims & Objectives

- To produce attractive products for the customer.

- To sell quality products at a cheap price.

- To develop environmental friendly products.

- To reduce the rate of carbon emissions.

- To expand its business in entire world.

- To create global clients and customers.

- To create job opportunity for the unemployed people.

- To make profit for the shareholders and rise its profit level.

Besides, the company maintain a Plan called 'Plan A', by which the company is trying to develop environmental friendly products and trying to reduce the rate of carbon emissions (Corporate.marksandspencer.com, 2015).

The ownership of M&S is mainly depended on the share. M&S is a public Ltd. Company, hence the ownership, liabilities are depended on the initial public offering, often through the Stock Exchange.

Although the company was established by the Michael Marks. He begun the business as a sole trader until in 1894. Then he started a partnership business with Tom Spencer, a former wholesale company owner. After sometimes the company expanded its business in UK and EU, at that time the company had been turned into public ltd. company.

2.3 The London School of Economics and Political Science (LSE)

The London School of Economics and Political Science (LSE) is one of the best public research University for the Business, economics and political science was established in 1895 (Wikipedia, 2015). It's a constituent college of the Federal University of London. The educational organization that offers different programs for its students such as Honors, Masters, Diploma etc. It's a non-profitable business organization that don't run for profit (Lse.ac.uk, 2015). The goal of this institution is to provide better and world class education to its students.

The organization is located at the central London, UK. The Organization was founded by Beatrice and Sidney Webb in 1895 (Wikipedia, 2015). LSE has been achieved rank 3rd in the Complete University Guide 2014 (Lse.ac.uk, 2015). And the institution is gradually improving its local and global university ranking. The endowment of this organization is £97.2m.

2.4 Aims & Objectives

The main motto of this institution is "To Know the Causes of Things" (Wikipedia, 2015). The organization is trying to follow this motto through their aims and objectives (Lse.ac.uk, 2015). The aims and objectives of this organization are as follows:

- To provide quality education for all the students.
- To establish research based education system.
- To develop business and economic education skills.
- To help the poor and meritorious students through the scholarship.
- To develop local and global political science related knowledge within the students.
- To help the other educational or research organizations in different works.
- To provide education at low cost.
- To spend the earnings of the institute for the development of the institution, students and teachers.
- To establish practical knowledge and research based education system.

As LSE is the constituent college of the Federal University of London, but the university is a self-funded university and also has a self-governance system (Lse.ac.uk, 2015). The organization is registered under the Company act and also registered under the Charity act 1993 (Wikipedia, 2015). The major governing bodies of this organization are:

- LSE Council
- The Court of Governors
- The Academic Board; and the Director and Director's Management Team

2.5 Influence of the Stake Holders

Stake holders are the person who're enjoying the profit and various facilities of the organization (UKEssays, 2015). These people are also liable for the breakdown or losses of the organization (Dransfield, 2014).

In the company and organizational business concepts, there are various types of stake holders are related to every business organization either it's profitable or non-profitable. But this stake holder process can be distinguished in two ways: 1. Internal Stake Holders and 2. External Stake Holders (Dransfield, 2014). Internal stake holders play a vital role in the development and growth of the business.

Employee, manager, Owners etc. are measured as the internal stake holders of an organization (Guy, 2009). On the other hand there are various types of external stake holders who're externally related to every business organization, namely suppliers, society, government, creditors, customers, consumers (Guy, 2009). Although consumer is considered as the major stake holders in the organizational business concepts. The following diagram can more clarify the concept of organizational business's stake holders:

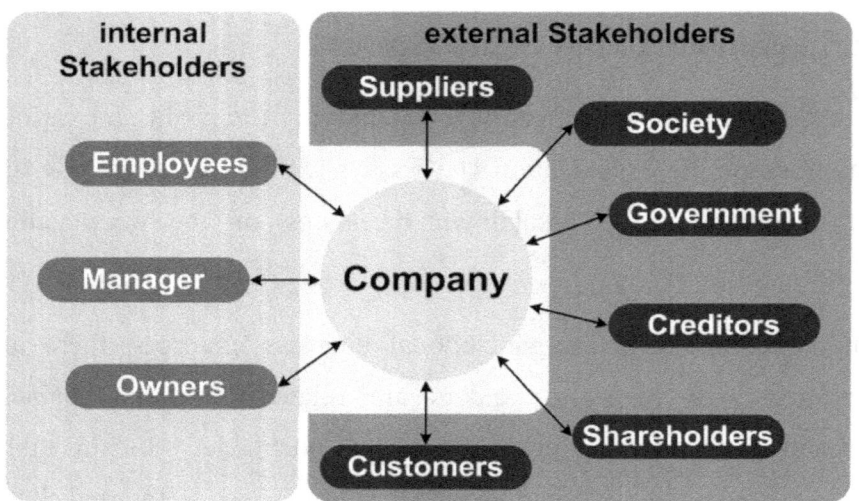

Figure 1: A diagram of various types of Stake holders

Marks & Spencer (M&S) always tries to satisfy their stake holders by providing different kinds of incentives. As the employee of M&S are liable for the development and growth of this business organization, hence the employees of the M&S get large sum of incentives in every year for their good performances (UKEssays, 2015).

Besides, M&S always tries to satisfy their owners, shareholders, suppliers, creditors by giving them the return of the investment in time. The business organization also provides different types of financial and logical support to the govt. to the development of the society (UKEssays, 2015).

In this point of view, the stake holders of the London School of Economics and Political Science (LSE) are totally different. It also has internal and external stake holders as well. But the internal stake holders of this organization are teachers, governing bodies of the institute and employee. And the external stake holders of this organization are students, suppliers, society and govt. (Lse.ac.uk, 2015).

The major stake holders of this organization is their students. Because the main objective of this organization isn't building profit instead the organization objective is to provide world class education for the students. The society and govt. are also included in this stake holders group, because LSE works for the betterment of the society and the county (Lse.ac.uk, 2015). The internal stake holders like the teachers, governing bodies of the institute, and employee of this organization get good incentives for their efforts. These person are related to the development of the organization.

3.0 Business Structure of the Organization

Every organization has a structure to obtain its goals and objectives. The organizational structure helps an organization to follow the command of the highest level and implement it by the lowest level to reach the common objectives of the organization. Like M&S and LSE, different types of organizations are used different kinds of organizational structure. There mainly five common types of organizational structure,

- Functional

- Divisional

- Matrix

- Process-Based

- Network

Discussion of Common Types of Organizational Structure

Structure Type	Description
Functional	Top-down, specialized departments reporting through separate chains of command, joined only at the top
Divisional	Each unit or division dedicated to one product, geographic area, common technology, or customer base
Matrix	Combination of functional and self-contained units, lateral teams imposed on functional departments
Process-Based	Process Owners drive team-based strategic execution with customer oriented goals in mission-based processes
Network	Separate units either internal or external to the company, each unit specializes in a business task or function held together by ad hoc arrangements

3.1 M&S Organizational Structure

M&S uses flat hierarchical organizational structure organizational structure, because this type of organizational structure has limited level of management between administrative level and front line employees. Due to the limited management level, the lower level employees of the M&S can easily communicate with the upper level top officials even CEO to solve any problem of the organization.

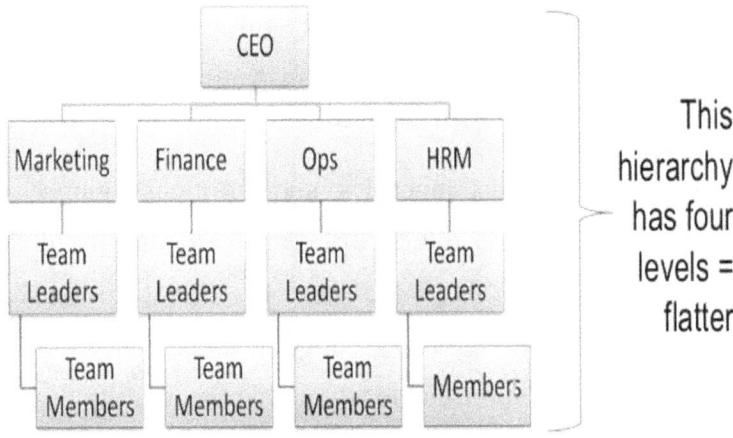

Figure 2: The flat organizational structure of Marks & Spencer (M&S)

This organizational structure of M&S assist the top level management to formulate any types of policy and implement the policy throughout the organization rapidly. As a multinational business organization, M&S nicely implements this organizational structure in the different sectors even the different operational fields of its business. The production, marketing and planning strategies of the business are totally depended on this organizational structure.

The flat organizational structure promote M&S to expand the plan or strategies of the organization very rapidly throughout the international offices of the organization. M&S has large number of employee force in the different geographical areas of the world, hence the flat organizational structure can reduce the authoritarian problem as well as reduce the overall cost and speed up the working process of the organization. Even the flat organizational structure can help the M&S to achieve the SMART objectives of the business.

3.2 LSE Organizational Structure

The London School of Economics and Political Science (LSE) organizational structure is totally different from the organizational structure of M&S. LSE maintains functional organizational structure. In this formation, every entity of the organization except the supreme one is the subordinate to a single other entity.

LSE uses this organizational structure to create a span of control in the every department of the organization. As an educational institution, this organizational structure assist the subordinate to create a strong bond with the top level management and the subordinate.

Although functional organizational structure is a costly structural concepts of business and the decision of the top level needs more time to reach boundary of the lower level. But LSE doesn't operate their business for making profit, hence the organization get more reliance in the SMART, strategically planning and controlling fields with the help of the hierarchical organizational structure.

LSE has top, mid and lower level organizational fields and the Chancellor (sometimes also referred to as 'Director') is the supreme governing body of the organization. Executive Vice chancellor (also referred to as Pro-Directors) are responsible for operating and controlling the different process of the organization such as, teaching, learning, research and planning.

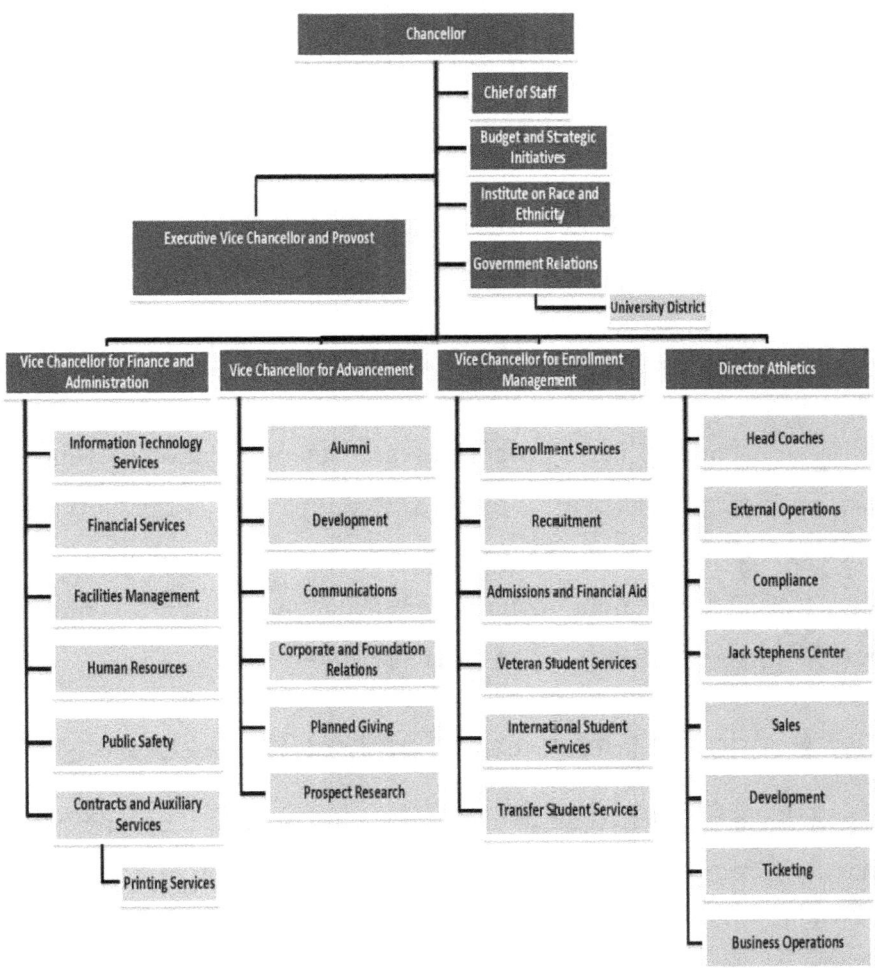

Figure 3: The organizational structure of London School of Economics and Political Science (LSE)

3.3 The Effect of Economic Environment

The economic environment can greatly affect the business environment of any organization. The economic environment of business is come from the economic environment of a country (International Monetary Fund, 1990). Inflation, GDP, interest rates etc. economic environments of a country can change the business environment of an organization (International Monetary Fund, 1990).

Now, we will show the impact of the different economic environments in the two different countries business organization's point of view. Suppose the one of this business organization is Marks & Spencer (M&S) of UK and the other one is Walmart of USA (Walmart.com, 2015).

Although both of these companies are the multinational company and operating their business in the different nations of the world. But they are depended on the economic environment of their mother countries. The different economic environment of the both countries and its impact on M&S and Walmart are given below:

3.4 Economic Environment of the UK and USA

The UK and USA economy have some similarity at the same time it have differences. UK has the second largest economy in Europe after Germany. In the recent years, the govt. of UK has been reduced the number of public owned business and increase its initiatives in social business and social welfare, so the per-capita GDP of UK has fallen down at $35,046.59.

Where, USA has a largest market oriented and technologically powerful economy. The per-capita GDP of USA is $49,800. The private individuals and business firms have made most of the economic decision of this country. The business firms of this country feel more flexibility than the business organization of Asia and EU. The economic table of UK and USA is as follows:

UK USA

	UK	USA	
Exports	$473.00 billion Ranked 10th.	$1.56 trillion Ranked 2nd. 3 times more than United Kingdom	
GDP	$2.44 trillion Ranked 7th.	$15.68 trillion Ranked 2nd. 6 times more than United Kingdom	
GDP > Composition by sector > Industry	21.1% Ranked 146th. 10% more than United States	19.1% Ranked 160th.	
GDP > Per capita	$35,046.59 per capita Ranked 21st.	$45,759.46 per capita Ranked 8th. 31% more than United Kingdom	
GDP > Per capita > PPP	$36,600.00 Ranked 21st.	$51,700.00 Ranked 6th. 41% more than United Kingdom	
GDP > Purchasing power parity	$2.31 trillion Ranked 8th.	$16.24 trillion Ranked 1st. 7 times more than United Kingdom	
GDP per capita	$38,514.46 Ranked 21st.	$49,965.27 Ranked 10th. 30% more than United Kingdom	
Gross National Income	$1.48 trillion Ranked 4th.	$9.78 trillion Ranked 1st. 7 times more than United Kingdom	
Inflation rate > Consumer prices	2.8% Ranked 126th. 33% more than United States	2.1% Ranked 160th.	
Population below poverty line	14% Ranked 18th.	15.1% Ranked 34th. 8% more than United Kingdom	
Public debt	88.7% of GDP Ranked 19th. 27% more than United States	70% of GDP Ranked 37th.	
Unemployment rate	8% Ranked 51st.	8.1% Ranked 47th. 1% more than United Kingdom	

Figure 4: The economic table of UK and USA

3.5 The impact of UK & USA Economic Environment on M&S and Walmart

After the end of recession in the year 2013, the GDP growth rate of UK is 1.7% and the GDP growth rate of USA is 2.2%. These rates suggest that the demand of domestic products in these countries are rising gradually and it will add more income in the Per-capita GDP.

So the business organization like M&S and Walmart will able to sell more products or services in the upcoming years to their local as well as the international customers.

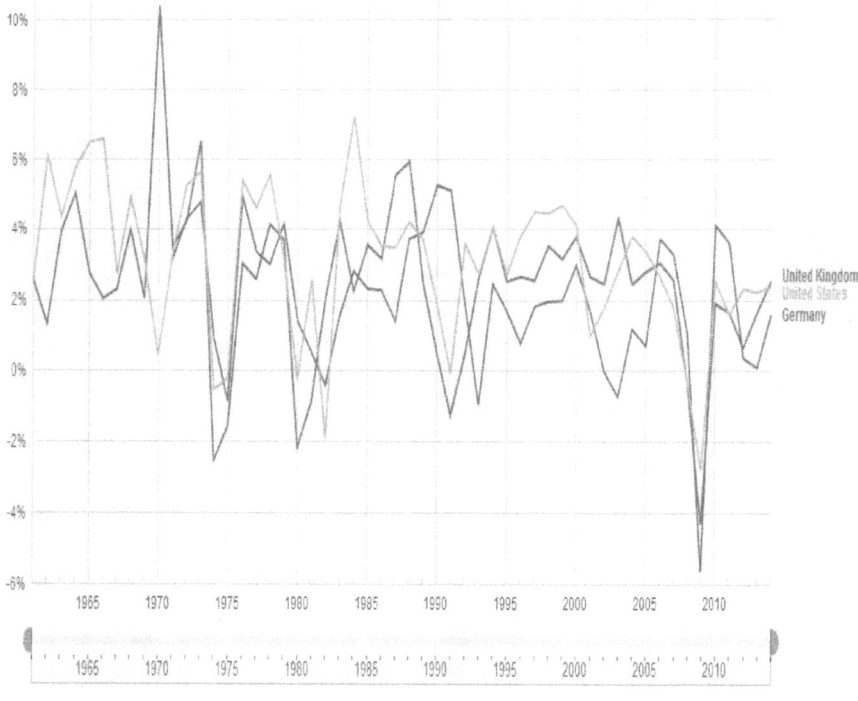

Figure 5: GDP growth Rate of UK, USA and Germany

Walmart will able to obtain more profit than M&S as the GDP growth rate of USA is better than the growth rate of UK. The inflation rate of UK is 2.8% which is quite more than the inflation rate of USA (Nationmaster.com, 2015). The govt. of UK has already taken some steps to control the flow of money in the market (Nationmaster.com, 2015). To control this inflation rate, the govt. of UK has increased the bank interest rate, hence it greatly impact on the economic environment of M&S.

Because of this increased interest rate M&S has reduced its loaning process from the banks, it also greatly affects their business growth. As the inflation rate of USA is 2.1% (Nationmaster.com, 2015), which is quite lower than the inflation rate of UK, hence it can't greatly impact on the Walmart's economic environment.

Walmart can easily expand their business by taking loan from the bank. Because the govt. of USA doesn't add excessive level of interest rate on the bank loan. But the economy of USA is gradually declining (Nationmaster.com, 2015), so Walmart can face economic crisis in the upcoming years.

In this point, the economy of UK is gradually developing, but the development process can be greatly effected after the competition of Brexit process. As the UK quits its membership from EU, thus the Multinational companies like M&S will face big challenges to operate its business in EU zone. For that reason, it can be tough for M&S to develop their business and increased their net profit in the upcoming years (Walmart.com, 2015).

4.0 McDonald' s and NHS Business Environment Analysis

4.1 McDonald' s

McDonald is one of the biggest food chain companies in the world which is serving a large number of customer worldwide on daily basis. McDonald's food quality, cleanliness, quick services and their everyday value added services has made it create a high brand image.

The highly developed operational system, modern infrastructure, customer driven policies and effective management has given McDonald's a better position to survive and sustain in the competitive market. In 1948, McDonald's was first started in the USA. With its foundation, it achieves its success. In the present market, McDonald is considered as one of the largest and reputed food service retailers' in the world.

McDonald operates mainly in the catering industry. It consists completely of restaurants preparing and serving a limited menu which is quickly arranged and sold at reasonable prices. The organization has 32000 of restaurants across 117 countries. McDonald is also providing job opportunities to a large number of unemployed people worldwide. The company also provides supports to the local community (Caprotti, 2012). The company is based on franchising administration. McDonald has certain agreement policies for providing franchise to the local companies.

The company aims to endow greater opportunity to the local organization for the better utilization of the brand depiction of McDonald so they can commission the total infrastructure involved in the business. McDonald has made strategies to lower the risk of the local organization for commissioning of the required amount.

4.2 National Health Service (NHS)

In 1948, National Health Service (NHS) was founded by the United Kingdom Labour government. It was created to replace the inefficient system of volunteer hospitals present during the World War II. The main idea behind the foundation of NHS was to provide good healthcare services to everyone in the UK regardless of wealth with few exceptions such as the charge for prescriptions, dental and optical services. National Health Services is world's oldest and biggest government paid health care system.

NHS services are free for the UK residents. NHS main principle is to meet the need of everyone, free at the delivery point and based on clinical need. Currently, 64.1 million individuals in the UK and 53.9 million individuals in England are receiving the free services provided by the NHS. The services provided by NHS covers everything from routine screenings to the treatment of life-threatening diseases (House, 2011). More than 1.6 million people have been employed by the NHS which makes its position in the top 5 world largest workforces.

The funding of NHS comes directly from the taxation. NHS receives ten times more amount of budget then the time of its launch. NHS budget spends over paying the staffs, drugs, other suppliers, building, equipment and other requirements.

4.3 Description of Meetings of the Objectives of the Various Stakeholders

The primary focus of every organization is to accomplish the different objectives of the stakeholders. For both organizations taken above have different stakeholders. Here, McDonald is considered for the explanation of the objectives of the various stakeholders. The top stakeholders of McDonald's are the customers and the employees. Other stakeholders are the investors, suppliers and the community (Anuradha Reddy and Akula, 2011). Consumers are the most important stakeholders as the whole profits of the respective organizations and the sustainability of the business totally depends upon the selling of the product and the deals or services offers by the company.

One of the most vital objectives of the organization is to provide better services and deals for the customers. It is very crucial for the company to provide best products for the customers to enhance the business. The primary focuses of McDonald are to develop customer's reliability in the services and the desired products, through which company can increase their productivity and can achieve excellent growth in the business.

Investor plays a key role for monitoring the management system of McDonald. Investors help the company to utilize the financial resources by the proper implementation of the raw materials in the business. McDonald aims to satisfy the need of the investors as they play a major role for the enhancement of the business. The two major strategies of McDonald for sustaining the business are to increase the value for the shareholders with the highest return of the capital. For the enhancement of the business, workers play a significant role. So it is very crucial to satisfying the employees for the development of the business.

The organization is connected with a large number of workers across the world. To satisfy the employees of the company, McDonald spends a large amount for the incentives of the employees (Dai, 2013). The company also provides increments to satisfy their employee's demands. McDonald plans activities as well as better opportunities for the proper motivation of the employees. Activities and opportunities provided by the company help the employees to enhance their quality of work for the company.

Suppliers are also major stakeholders of McDonald. They provide various important goods and raw materials to the company. For Mc Donald, it is very important to satisfy the requirements of the suppliers. McDonald focuses on excellent transaction system between the company and the suppliers. It helps to create a better relationship between the company and different suppliers which in turn helps to enhance the business (Ngui, Warner and Weiss Roberts, 2015). Communities are one of the stakeholders of the organization. The company provides support to the communities by introducing Corporate Social Responsibility (CSR) program.

4.4 Responsibilities of Stakeholders

The organization aims to provide better products and services as per the requirements and satisfaction of the customers, but customers also have some of the necessary responsibilities towards the company. Customers should provide proper and accurate feedback to the company regarding the products and services provided by the Mc Donald. So the company can prepare strategies related to the feedback provided by the customers which will help in developing the business (Adam and Shavit, 2008).

The corporation provides all the relevant information regarding the company to their shareholders so the maximization of the profitability ratio can be achieved. For the growth of the company, responsibilities of shareholders are very important as they help the company by the proper execution of the work.

The most important responsibility of the employees of McDonald is to provide efficient work and to sustain workflow for the company. Efficient workforce by the employees will help the company to achieve the desired business. Suppliers' responsibility is to help McDonald by fulfilling the demands of raw materials at a correct time. Suppliers should obey all the laws, follows the best practice and should respect the environmental conditions.

4.5 Business Area of the Organization

McDonald is one of the most successful and performing extremely well in the present global competitive market. The corporation works acceding to the satisfactory needs of the customers with the better quality of foods and products at affordable prices. The managing structure of the organization is very effective and well-organized for maintaining the brand name of the organization.

Throughout the overall development process, the implementation of effectual business strategies according to the business structure can be easily identified. The business structure of this organization is mainly based on the geographical structure. The organization divided its operational activity into five geographical zones. According to the research, 75% of the total revenue is generated from the region of the United States and Europe. Therefore, the most significant strategic approach for the improvement of the organization is to keep their major market with expanding their market to the emerging regions. The organization earns their revenue as an operator of the restaurant, as an investor and as a franchise restaurant (Smith, 1999). The tactical approach of the organization is somewhat different form the existing fast food chains.

Apart from this, the revenue from franchises and marketing are calculated on the basis of sales percentage. However, the requirement and taste of the customers are different for the different group of the customer on the global platform. The geographical bodies are more concern about the response of the local customers. The production and marketing strategies based on the local requirement helps in sustainable development process. Apart from this, the philosophy of the organization has added a passion for enhancing the brand image. The excellent quality of food, services and cleanliness with collaborate management system has enhanced the future prospect of the organization (Dyllick and Muff, 2015).

The NHS was initiated with a purpose of good healthcare to all, in spite of wealth. The fundamental scheme of this organization is to meet the needs of the clinical patients. This provision to common people is complimentary at the point of delivery. The core principles and values of the organization help to sustain effectively for more than 60 years. The organization is an autonomous body and policies of strategic leadership are governed by the Department of Health. The organization is responsible for developing outcomes and quality of healthcare at the national level. Apart from national issues, the organization also operates clinical commissioning groups and allocates resources overseas.

4.6 Organizational Response on Market forces

The market forces are accountable for the various organizational responses. There is a variety of market forces, operating opportunities and challenges addressed by these organizations in their development process. It is essential for the organizations to identify the information demand, customer responsiveness and cost pressure.

In addition, a quick anticipation of the customer requirements helps these two corporations to continue sustainably in this competitive world. Supply and demand are an essential element for the survival of an organization in the competitive platform. The McDonald and NHS are performing excellently in these criteria for satisfying the demand of the customer. It operating function plays a significant role in the effective evaluation of the business.

Customer's sensitivity and action are two basic elements in determining the price of the product in the market. The prices of the products are prior to change with the quality of the product or services. The organizations are successful in retaining their customers by maintaining their extensive quality of products and services. The Economic level is also an important aspect from company's perspective as it helps in maintaining the reliability of the product and enhances the growth of the company.

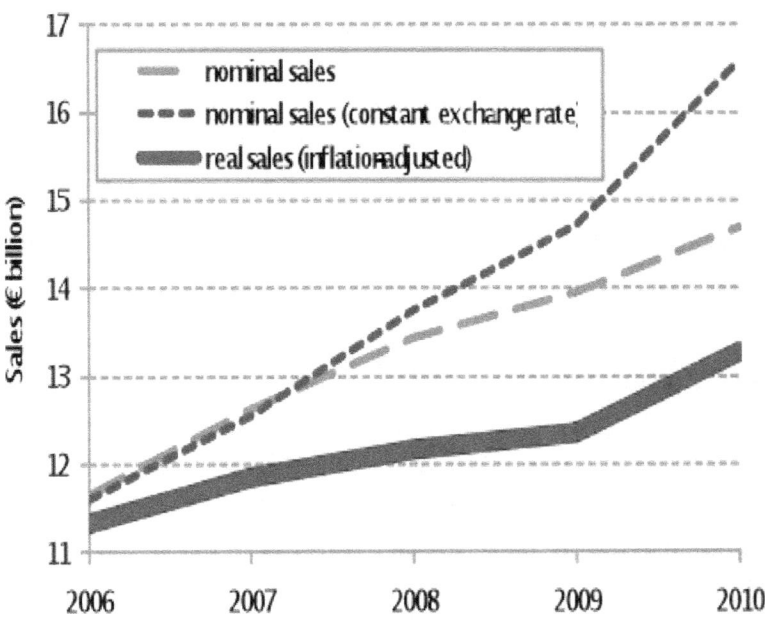

Figure 6: McDonald Sales graph in UK

4.7 Market Structures in Determination of Pricing of the Product & Services

Monopoly Market Structure

In the case of a monopoly market, the alteration in the profitability in the competitive market is significant for the business operation. Pricing of the products and services is not associated to the satisfying demands of the customers, and therefore, overall profitability ratio can be easily increased.

Oligopoly Market Structure

The market structure is related to the pricing as well as demands for the goods with that of the customers. Proper analysis and implementation of creativity of are essential for the growth of the business in the market. The McDonald and NHS implemented certain innovative strategies and policies, which helped the organization to extend sustainably on the global platform.

Perfect Competition Market

The business operation of McDonald group is rising significantly in the competitive market, and the company is involved in providing best suitable prices for the desired products to the respective customers.

4.8 The Effect of Economic Environment

The Economic Environment plays a significant role in the process of development of the business organization. The research aims to analyse and investigate the different economic factors that affect the operation of McDonald in the England and KFC in China. The research will also put light on the different strategic recommendations for the improvement of business effectiveness in a profitable way. McDonald operates a very complex system business environment on the global platform, which is extensively influenced by the economic process of the country. The economic climate of a country affects availability and price of raw material and labour, market brand, customer footsteps.

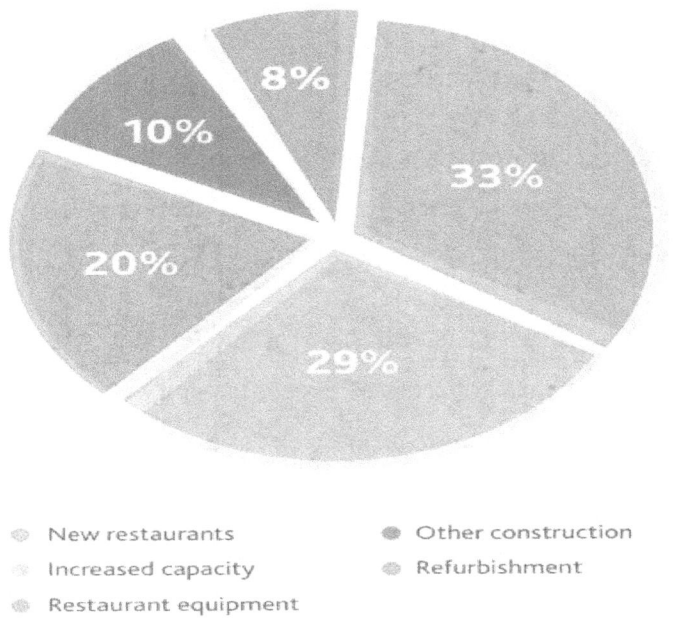

Figure 7: McDonald's Capital Investment in the UK

4.9 Economic Environment of the United Kingdom & China

The economic arrangement creates a great impact on the suitable allocation of the respective resources as per the suitability of the corporation. The governing bodies of UK and China get involved in controlling all the resources and relevant information for the regulatory authorities in this particular system of economic.

Due to lack of the proper amount of knowledge, the desired resources were not properly, allocated to the respective authorities. There are some of the minor difficulties caused to the company by the shortage of appropriate inputs. According to latest UK economic position, the GDP will continue at a stable pace in 2015 and 2016. According to a research, the UK market has slowed a slight but the domestic demand has increased.

The average GDP growth is 2.4% in the recent years. In the global economic scenario, China has become a recognised economic muscle and plays an essential role in global affairs.

The economic growth is slowing down due to tightening the policies of credit growth and lowering of excess capacity. The government is taking initiatives in short-term growth achievements (Kelly and Scott, 2011). The emerging economy of China is reflecting higher opportunities for global market investments.

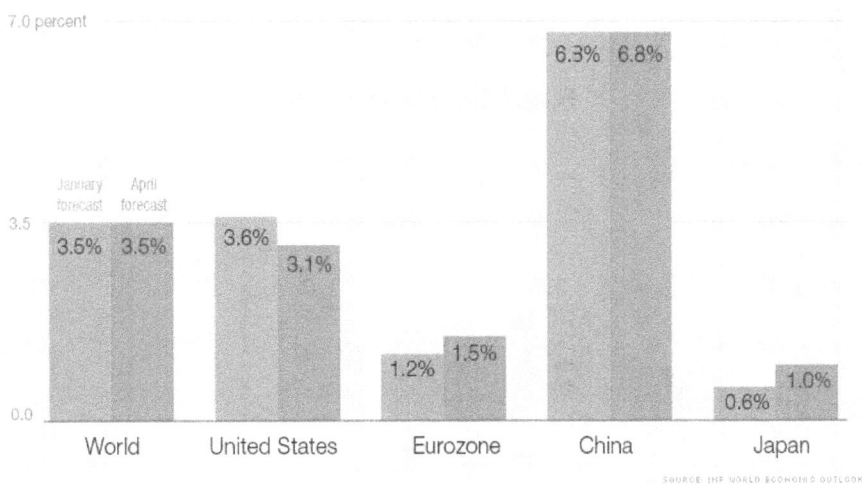

Figure 8: Economic Growth graph

4.10 Enterprise and Mixed Economic System

With the help of this particular section, the organization can execute the work efficiently which will help to the overall success of the organization. Suitable allocation of the resources is very crucial, as the competition is very tough in the market. Therefore, the proper allocation of the respective resources is very important for the business as it plays a crucial part in achieving the success for the company.

McDonald and KFC groups are greatly involved in understanding the demands of the customers, and they are functioning as per the suitability and satisfaction of the customers (Klasen, 2012). Thus, the overall system of enterprise economic system is very functional in managing the position of the corporation in the existing competitive market of UK and China

Real GDP Growth

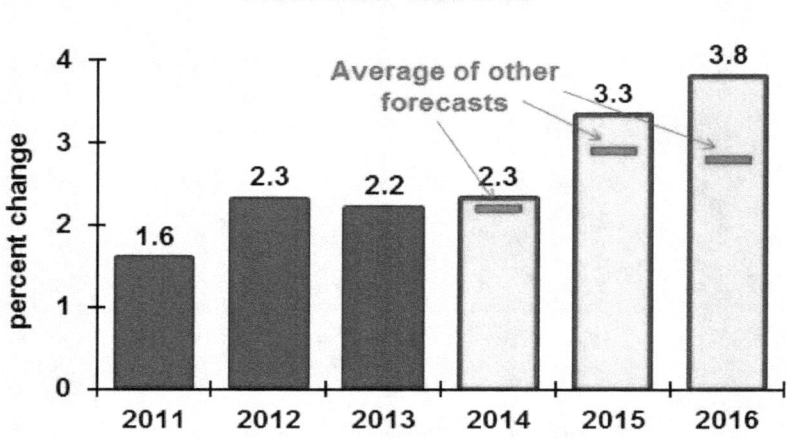

Figure 9: Real GDP growth of UK

4.11 Impact of Fiscal and Monetary Policies on the Business Organization

For maintaining effective control over the organization, there are some fiscal policies by the regulatory authorities as well as by the government, which helps to maintain the proper evaluation of the work of the company. The variation in the interest rate is emphasised by the monetary policies of the authorities which influences the business operation of the organization.

The development of new monetary policies by the UK governing authority helps to develop a new business model by the corporation.

The corporation provides a huge contribution to the economy of UK through a continuous network of restaurant investment. The overall amount of contribution of McDonald to the UK economy is about £2.5 billion annually. Therefore, change in the interest rate will affect the financial support of the organization by the increase in the capital cost and reduction in the volume of the overall sales. On the other hand, the fluctuation ratio of the interest rate is little lower which enhance the business environment of KFC in China (CONTRIBUTIONS ON ECONOMIC GROWTH, 2011).

The variable exchange rate as a result of innovative and advanced monetary policies has both positive and adverse effect on the business operation of the organizations. The development of new monetary policies by the UK and China by the respective authorities has influenced the financial balance of the organizations.

The tax rate distinction plays a significant role in the process of productivity and profitability of the organization in China. Therefore, the economic environment of KFC in China has an added privilege to utilise the market capital for the overall development process of the organization (Cizaire, 2014).

5.0 The Impact of Various Factors in the Development of Business Environment

The business environments of the organization are greatly influenced by the different factors. The major influential factors are Social, Political. Legal and Economic Factors. These are disused in the light of M&S, Walmart, and McDonald:

5.1 Social Factors

The social factors are greatly affecting the business environment of the companies like M&S and Walmart (Walmart.com, 2015). The promotional activities of the business organizations are also depended on the social factors. The different test and choices of the customers are also depended on the social factors of the country. As Walmart and M&S are operating their business in the different countries, so it should keep in mind that social factors can greatly impact on their business environments.

On the other hand, McDonald operates in different countries. Every country has its own culture and tradition. This change affects the business of McDonald. A customer expects the highest level of services and all the latest facilities from McDonald. To reach the expectation of the customers, McDonald needs to research the market effectively.

5.2 Political & Legal Factors

A political factor has a huge impact over the business operation. The four major effects of political factors over the business organizations impact on the economy, political stability, changes in regulation and mitigation of risk.

M&S and Walmart both are multinational business organization, these companies has different plans and policies to cope with the different political situations of the different countries of the worlds. Even the govt. created legal environment can create barriers to expand or develop business in the different countries. Political stability is the main concern for these sorts of business organizations.

Because unstable political situation hampers the growth of business. Hence, Walmart and M&S shouldn't select those country for the business, which political situation is unstable. Even the change of govt. or new law can create barriers for business (Hubbard and O'Brien, 2008). M&S and Walmart have to be prepared for these types of situations. For example, UK govt. has been formulated a law that increased the cost of hiring staff, in this situation M&S has reduced the rate of recruitment in their organization. They also have terminated some unskilled employees from their organization to cope with this legal situation.

However, McDonald's under the control of government's set of laws and policy (Belz, 2013). Several government policies can affect the business of McDonald. A change in the policies made by the government plays a crucial role in the business organization. The main issues regarding McDonald are the employee laws, tax issues and the license. McDonald follows both the local government's policies and foreign investment policies for the franchise business strategy. McDonald business is greatly influenced by the political instability of local state. McDonalds greatly affected by the change in the government as well as the policy changes made by the government.

Over the years, McDonald is facing different challenges on the legal issues in the different countries. The organization establishes different business plans to avoid litigations in the external and internal aspects of the organization (Mohamed, 2015). In some cases, the organizations are founded against certain scenario leading to fines and penalties. Therefore, in the UK it is essential to follow certain policies and rules to run operation successfully. It is mandatory for the organization in the UK to follow the rules regarding taxes, safety rules, registrations and stuff laws.

5.3 Economic Factors

Economic factors are very crucial for the business organization. McDonald operates in different countries and hence it faces different tax scale and revenue system (Yılmaz, 2013). The factors can greatly affect the business environment of the companies like M&S and Walmart. M&S and Walmart are operating their business is the different countries (Hubbard and O'Brien, 2008). If the economic conditions of those countries are fallen down then the companies like Walmart or M&S also has been fallen to economic crisis.

Because the purchasing power of the customers is mainly depended on the economic environment of a country. Economic debt, economic rescission, High rates of interest or Tax can breakdown the growth of the organization. So M&S and Walmart have to prepare new plans or policies to get rid of these major economic crisis.

However, the major difficulty faced by McDonald is the intercontinental currency value variation mainly in case of global food distribution. McDonald business is also affected by the local economic condition.

References

Adam, A. and Shavit, T. (2008). Roles and responsibilities of boards of directors revisited in reconciling conflicting stakeholders interests while maintaining corporate responsibility. *Journal of Management & Governance*, 13(4), pp.281-302.

Anuradha Reddy, M. and Akula, R. (2011). Corporate Governance - The Role of Various Stakeholders.*Prabandhan: Indian Journal of Management*, 4(5), p.50.

Baye, M. (2000). *Managerial economics & business strategy*. Boston: Irwin/McGraw-Hill.

Belz, F. (2013). Shaping the future: Sustainable innovation and entrepreneurship. *Social Business*, 3(4), pp.311-324.

Caprotti, F. (2012). Environment, Business and the Firm. *Geography Compass*, 6(3), pp.163-174.

Cizaire, C. (2014). Pricing: The third business skill: Principles of price management. *Journal of Revenue and Pricing Management*, 13(4), pp.339-340.

CONTRIBUTIONS ON ECONOMIC GROWTH. (2011). *Journal of Economic Surveys*, 25(5), pp.829-832.

Corporate.marksandspencer.com, (2015). *Our Plans for the Future*. [online] Available at: http://corporate.marksandspencer.com/aboutus/our-plans-for-the-future [Accessed 14 Dec. 2015].

Dransfield, R. (2014). *Business economics*. London: Routledge.

Dai, D. (2013). Cooperative economic growth. *Economic Modelling*, 33, pp.407-415.

Dyllick, T. and Muff, K. (2015). Clarifying the Meaning of Sustainable Business: Introducing a Typology from Business-as-Usual to True Business Sustainability. *Organization & Environment*.

Guy, F. (2009). The global environment of business. Oxford: Oxford University Press.

Hopkins, M. (2003). *The planetary bargain*. London: Earthscan Publications.

Hubbard, R. and O'Brien, A. (2008). *Economics*. Upper Saddle River, N.J.: Pearson Prentice Hall.

House, J. (2011). UK National Health Service reforms mobilise doctors. *The Lancet*, 377(9768), pp.797-800.

International Monetary Fund, (1990). Public Policy and the Enviroment: Survey of the Literature. *IMF Working Papers*, 90(56), p.1.

Kelly, S. and Scott, D. (2011). Relationship benefits: Conceptualization and measurement in a business-to-business environment. *International Small Business Journal*, 30(3), pp.310-339.

Klasen, A. (2012). Generating Economic Growth - How Governments can help successfully. *Global Policy*, 3(2), pp.238-241.

Lse.ac.uk, (2015). *About LSE - About LSE - Home.* [online] Available at: http://www.lse.ac.uk/aboutLSE/aboutHome.aspx [Accessed 14 Dec. 2015].

Mohamed, A. (2015). The international business environment: a proposed analytical framework.*International Journal of Business Environment*, 7(2), p.168.

Nationmaster.com, (2015). *United Kingdom vs United States: Economy Facts and Stats.* [online] Available at: http://www.nationmaster.com/country-info/compare/United-Kingdom/United-States/Economy [Accessed 14 Dec. 2015].

Ngui, E., Warner, T. and Weiss Roberts, L. (2015). Ethical Responsibilities and Perceptions of Stakeholders of Genetic Research Involving Racial/Ethnic Minority Participants. *AJOB Empirical Bioethics*, 6(3), pp.15-27.

Smith, G. (1999). The UK National Health Service and the national health: 1948-98. *Critical Public Health*, 9(1), pp.69-74.

UKEssays, (2015). Marks And Spencers Organizational Structure Business Essay. [online] Available at: http://www.ukessays.com/essays/business/marks-and-spencers-organizational-structure-business-essay.php [Accessed 14 Dec. 2015].

Walmart.com, (2015). Walmart. [online] Available at: http://www.walmart.com/ [Accessed 14 Dec. 2015].

Wikipedia, (2015). London School of Economics. [online] Available at: https://en.wikipedia.org/wiki/London_School_of_Economics [Accessed 14 Dec. 2015].

Yılmaz, E. (2013). Competition, taxation and economic growth. *Economic Modelling*, 35, pp.134-139.

About the Author

Ghazi Mokammel Hossain is a professional e-book, article, research, analysis paper and a creative writer. He has written some books as well as many articles, research papers, analysis and creative articles. The author is also a freelance writer as well as a researcher. He was born on 31 December, 1993. He has passed his S.S.C exam from Dhaka under Dhaka Board in 2008 and passed his H.S.C exam from Dhaka under Dhaka Board in 2010. He has graduated with a Bachelor's of Business Administration in HRM in 2015 from a renowned University. He has also completed Computer Science and Engineering certificate course in 2011.

He published his first book called "IPv4 IP6 Technology & Implementation" in Amazon Kindle and Createspace on 2013. The author published his second book called "Introduction to Network on Chip Routing Algorithms" in 2014. He also published "Fundamental of API Based Financial Engineering" and "Ebola Epidemic: A Detail Survival Guide From Ebola Virus Disease Outbreak" in 2014. The author published an outstanding thrilling novel called "The Survival of USA" in 2016 on Amazon kindle and Createspace. Playing football, Cricket, PC games, reading books, novel, research paper, cycling and mountain climbing are his favorite hobbies.

- Business Environment: Theoretical & Organizational Aspects – July, 2016 by Ghazi Mokammel Hossain

- The Survival of USA - Part One: A Novel – March, 2016 by Ghazi Mokammel Hossain, MD. Fazle Mubin & Pranjal Rahman

- Enterprise IPv6 for Enterprise Networks- December, 2015 by Ghazi Mokammel Hossain & Fathe Mubin

- Heart of Democracy: A Versatile Poetry Book - Aug 28, 2015 by Ghazi Mozammel Hossain

- The Brave Parrot of Jungle - Dec 11, 2014 by Syeda Taskin Ara & Gulshan Ahmed

- IPv4 IPv6 Technology and Implementaticn - Nov 2, 2013 by Ghazi Mokammel Hossain & GM Hossain

- The Mirror of Religion - Jul 19, 2015 by Ghazi Mozammel Hossain & Richard Marks

- Introduction to Network on Chip Routing Algorithms - Oct 4, 2014 by Ghazi Mokammel Hcssain

- Ebola Epidemic: A Detail Survival Guide From Ebola Virus Disease Outbreak - Oct 25, 2014 by Ghazi Mokammel Hossain & Dr. Robert Alex

- Fundamental of API Based Financial Engineering - Oct 17, 2014 by Ghazi Mokammel Hossain

For more details please visit Amazon Author Central
amazon.com/author/ghazimokammelhossain